Proverbs
Wisdom for the Whole of Life

A six-session Bible study for individuals and small groups

By Antony Billington

Blessed are those who find wisdom, those who gain understanding, for she is more profitable than silver and yields better returns than gold. *She is more precious than rubies; nothing you desire can compare with her.*

Proverbs 3:13-15

INTER-VARSITY PRESS
36 Causton Street, London SW1P 4ST, England
Email: ivp@ivpbooks.com
Website: www.ivpbooks.com

First published 2019

British Library Cataloguing-in-Publication Data
A catalogue record for this book is available from the British Library

ISBN: 978–1–78974–082–0
eBook ISBN: 978–1–78974–083–7

Typeset in Great Britain by Sublime
Print and production managed in Great Britain by Jellyfish Print Solutions

*Inter-Varsity Press publishes Christian books that are true to the Bible
and that communicate the gospel, develop discipleship and strengthen
the church for its mission in the world.*

*IVP originated within the Inter-Varsity Fellowship, now the Universities
and Colleges Christian Fellowship, a student movement connecting
Christian Unions in universities and colleges throughout Great Britain,
and a member movement of the International Fellowship of Evangelical
Students. Website: www.uccf.org.uk. That historic association is
maintained, and all senior IVP staff and committee members subscribe to
the UCCF Basis of Faith.*

Contents

The Gateway Seven

Exodus — Law

Ezekiel — Prophecy

Mark — Gospel

1 Peter — Letters

Proverbs — Wisdom

Revelation — Apocalyptic

Ruth — Narrative

The Gateway Seven Bible Study Series

We don't approach a novel in the same way we tackle a legal document. We don't read poetry in the same way we might read a letter from a friend. So, we don't read the 66 books of the Bible as if they were all the same kind of writing. Story, song, law, letter, and more, all make up the rich repository of writing that together is God's word to us.

For *The Gateway Seven* series we've selected seven books of the Bible that each represent a different kind of writing. The mini-features sprinkled through the studies, together with the questions suggested for discussion, invite you to explore each book afresh in a way that's sensitive to its genre as well as to the concerns of the book itself.

Each study engages with a different kind of writing. However, each one in the series has been crafted with the same central desire: to offer a gateway to a deeper love of God's word and richer insights into its extraordinary implications for all of life, Monday through Sunday.

'May your kingdom come – on earth as in heaven', Jesus taught us to pray. May your kingdom come in our homes and places of work and service. May your kingdom come at the school gate as well as in the sanctuary. May your kingdom come in the hydrotherapy pool, in the council chamber, on the estate, around the Board table. May your kingdom come as we learn to live our everyday lives as beloved sons and daughters, wondrously wrapped up in our Father's 'family business'.

Our prayer is that these seven distinctive books of the Bible will be a gateway for you to a richer, deeper, transforming life with God wherever you are – seven days a week.

Tracy Cotterell
The Gateway Seven Series Editor
Managing Director - Mission, LICC

Making the Most of Proverbs

Introduction to Proverbs
Wisdom for the Whole of Life

The flood of 'how to' and 'self-help' books, magazine columns, and blogs – on everything from work to relationships to money to children – says something about our collective sense of lack of wisdom for everyday situations. Life can be confusing, and we want help to navigate it well.

In an expression of what lies at the heart of the gospel – God taking the loving initiative to respond to our need – the book of Proverbs reminds us that God has not left us alone to steer through life as best we can. Here, if we will respond to the invitation given, is wisdom to guide us through the delights and demands of everyday living. Proverbs makes it clear that wisdom doesn't begin in human autonomy, but in relationship with God, where wisdom is then worked out in different spheres of life – in our homes and our workplaces, our neighbourhoods and communities – wherever God has called us.

Here is a book populated with the types of people we are, and the types of people we encounter most days – adolescents and parents, spouses and friends, colleagues and clients, the gullible and the lazy, the old and the young, those who might lead us astray and those who help us stay on track.

Here is a book which knows that life is lived in seasons as well as in days and hours, in relationship with others, and on specific frontlines – those everyday places where we spend most of our time.

Here is a book to remind us that following Jesus is connected to the whole of life, a book which provides guidance for living wisely in God's world, which not only encourages us to make wise choices, but develops our character as we read it and seek to live it out.

Here is a book which stands as a reminder of the availability of wisdom from God for every situation as we make our way through life. Indeed, the Bible reminds us that if any of us lacks wisdom, we can ask God, 'who gives generously to all without finding fault', and it will be given to us (James 1:5). The good news is that God offers wisdom for us, for the whole of life.

An excellent 8-minute animated overview of the book of Proverbs has been produced by **The Bible Project** at jointhebibleproject.com or search YouTube for: 'Read Scripture: Proverbs'

Studying Proverbs

This Bible Study is designed to look at select passages in Proverbs over six sessions:

Session 1 | A Lord to Honour (Proverbs 1:1-7)

Session 2 | A Path to Take (Proverbs 2:1-22)

Session 3 | A Choice to Make (Proverbs 9:1-18)

Session 4 | A Life to Pursue (Proverbs 15:16-33)

Session 5 | A Way to Speak (Proverbs 10:18-21; 11:11-13; 25:11-15; 26:17-22)

Session 6 | A Model to Follow (Proverbs 31:10-31)

You can work through each session on your own, one-to-one, or in a small group.

If your church's preaching is covering Proverbs, this study is an ideal way to deepen your understanding and explore the passages' implications for your frontline - the place where you spend a significant amount of time during the week. Working through the sessions in a group also encourages each of you to share your insights and stories of God at work with others.

Each group has its own way of doing things, so the session plan is a suggestion, not a rule.

Suggested session plan

—

1 Pray to open

2 Read the 'First Thoughts' section

3 Read the passage from Proverbs

4 Work through the questions

The questions cover different areas - the session's main theme, what the Bible passage says and means, going deeper, and living out the passage. Many questions don't have 'right' or 'wrong' answers. It's important and helpful to hear insights from everyone in the group. Group leaders may want to pick out the most pertinent questions for their group to discuss.

5 Pray to close

Don't feel bound by these prayer prompts if your study has taken a different turn. Be flexible in responding to each other's needs.

Dotted throughout this guide are brief feature pieces on questions or issues related to the background and study of Proverbs. Together with some real-life stories – lived examples of how God's word can be worked out in daily life – they offer insights to deepen our understanding of the book and its implications.

Names and identifying details of the stories in this book have been changed to maintain anonymity.

Participating in the study

Before each session, you might like to read the passage together with one of the features, and any explanation boxes or stories that accompany the session. After you meet, you might like to pursue some of the 'Going Deeper' questions on your own.

Use this space to

Note down one or two things that strike you. As you journey through the study, come back to these notes each time and reflect on what God has been teaching you.

My frontline

Before you start the study, reflect on your frontline using these questions. Your frontline is an everyday place where you live, work, study, or play and where you're likely to connect with people who aren't Christians.

Where is your frontline?

What's going on there?
Who's with you there?

What are you excited about or struggling with?

What opportunities or challenges are you facing?

Come back to this reflection throughout the sessions, praying and trusting that God will direct your ways through his word.

Reading the whole of Proverbs on your own

Alongside the main sessions in this book, you may want to read through more of Proverbs on your own. The following are three possible reading plans, along with questions and thoughts to guide your personal reflections.

Read a chapter a day

Some people make a habit of reading a chapter of Proverbs every day, one for every day of the month. Such a practice can be very helpful, and you may want to try to do that for as long as your church or small group is studying the book. As you do so, note what strikes you or any questions that are raised.

Spend six weeks in Proverbs 10–29

Alternatively, you could focus your reading on smaller sections of the individual sayings in Proverbs 10–29, using the reading guide on the facing page. Each week has six readings (use the seventh day to take a rest or catch up!). Read through each section slowly, perhaps twice. Pick a few proverbs which stand out to you and ask:

- How does this issue relate to my life today/this week?

- What things do I need to take note of?

- How far do I see this trait in myself or in others?

- How do I want to pray?

Use a year-long devotional

The Way of Wisdom: A Year of Daily Devotions in the Book of Proverbs by Timothy and Kathy Keller (London: Hodder & Stoughton, 2017) is a helpful devotional resource on Proverbs designed to last a year with a reflection and prayer for every day.

Whatever scheme works best for you, before starting your study reflect on what is happening on your frontline - use the worksheet on page 15. Come back to your answers throughout your study. When you get to the end, reflect on the journey you've taken, and how far you've grown in confidence, insight, and wisdom.

Six-week reading scheme for Proverbs 10–29

Week 1

- 10:1–11
- 10:12–21
- 10:22–32
- 11:1–15
- 11:16–12:4
- 12:5–15

Week 2

- 12:16–28
- 13:1–11
- 13:12–25
- 14:1–15
- 14:16–27
- 14:28–35

Week 3

- 15:1–15
- 15:16–33
- 16:1–19
- 16:20–33
- 17:1–19
- 17:20–18:4

Week 4

- 18:5–21
- 18:22–19:14
- 19:15–20:4
- 20:5–21:8
- 21:9–19
- 21:20–22:5

Week 5

- 22:6–16
- 22:17–23:18
- 23:19–24:22
- 24:23–34
- 25:1–20
- 25:21–26:12

Week 6

- 26:13–28
- 27:1–22
- 27:23–28:11
- 28:12–28
- 29:1–11
- 29:12–27

Session 1

A Lord to Honour

Proverbs 1:1–7

First Thoughts

How should I live my life?

Judging by the ever-expanding self-help sections in bookshops and proliferation of lifestyle gurus, blogs, and social media feeds, it's a question many people are asking. Perhaps your friends and colleagues are. Perhaps you are.

We're aware we're not the best we can be. We need wisdom. Given our need, it would be all too easy to turn the book of Proverbs into a set of principles for living or a moralistic list of dos and don'ts. In fact, it's a profoundly gospel-shaped book in which God does for us what we couldn't do for ourselves. He takes the loving initiative to address our need for wisdom to live well in his world. The book puts God at the heart of our lives, not us. Where we can sometimes see ourselves as the centre of our own personal universe, with God somewhere at the periphery, dropping in every now and then when we need him to do so, Proverbs tells us that he is at the centre of all things, that we find true wisdom only in relationship with him and reverence of him.

Read – Proverbs 1:1-7

¹The proverbs of Solomon son of David, king of Israel: ² for gaining wisdom and instruction; for understanding words of insight; ³ for receiving instruction in prudent behaviour, doing what is right and just and fair; ⁴ for giving prudence to those who are simple, knowledge and discretion to the young – ⁵ let the wise listen and add to their learning, and let the discerning get guidance – ⁶ for understanding proverbs and parables, the sayings and riddles of the wise. ⁷ The fear of the LORD is the beginning of knowledge, but fools despise wisdom and instruction.

Focus on the Theme

1. As you start these studies, what is it you need wisdom for?

Perhaps spend some time sharing with each other an issue or question, big or small, you're facing right now – a tricky season at work, a complex family scenario, a relationship that needs attention, a non-Christian friend you're concerned for, an opportunity you're unsure whether to take. Consider writing this down and come back to it periodically as you go through the studies, or at the end, to see whether and how it has been addressed by your time spent in the book of Proverbs.

What Does the Bible Say?

2. In what ways does Proverbs 1:1 put us in touch with the larger biblical story?

3. How does Proverbs 1:2-4 describe the purposes of the book?

4. The bulk of chapters 1–9 appears to be addressed to a young man starting out in adult life, but in what ways does this opening of the book (especially 1:4-5) broaden the audience to include others?

5. What might 'fear of the LORD' (1:7) mean?

Look at some other references to this elsewhere in the book – 1:29; 2:5; 3:7; 8:13; 9:10; 10:27; 14:2, 16, 26-27; 15:16, 33; 16:6; 19:23; 22:4; 23:17; 24:21; 31:30.

Divide verses between pairs or threes depending on the size of the group, and report back any findings on what the fear of the Lord involves.

The fear of the Lord – relationship and reverence

———

The 'fear of the LORD' is a motif which runs through the Bible's wisdom literature, not just in Proverbs, but in Job and Ecclesiastes too (Job 28:28; Ecclesiastes 5:7; 12:13-14). To our ears, the word 'fear' can suggest a sense of cringing terror or dread, but that's probably not intended here – though there is a level of 'fear and trembling' that is appropriate when faced with the presence of God. The English words 'awe' or 'reverence' perhaps come closest to what is implied in most uses of the word. If wisdom literature is concerned with living wisely in God's world, then the fear of the Lord is the first principle of such a life, where being wise finds its foundation in a relationship with, and a deep reverence of, the covenant Lord God, rather than being wise in one's own eyes (cf. Proverbs 3:7). This then shapes the decisions we make in everyday life and directs our prayers as we seek to grow in wisdom.

Going Deeper

6. The connection between the king and wisdom (1:1) is also found in the description in Isaiah 11:1-3 of a future king. What characteristics does he share with those listed in Proverbs 1:2-7?

7. The association between the king and wisdom comes to its climax in Jesus, the wisdom of God. But if Jesus is 'greater than Solomon' (Matthew 12:42), does that make the book of Proverbs redundant for Christians today? Why or why not?

Living it Out

8. Think back to the issue or question you raised in the first question above. How might the qualities of 'prudence... knowledge and discretion' (1:4) be applicable in this situation?

9. According to this passage, wisdom combines intellectual, moral, and practical skills. Which of these would you like to grow in on your frontline, and why?

10. What things in everyday life might we be tempted to 'fear' instead of the Lord? How does our complete adoration and awe of God help deal with those other fears?

Prayer Time

- Draw on the words and ideas of Proverbs 1:1-17 to pray for your group.

- Pray for each other in the light of the issues shared at the start of the session, expressing trust that God will enable you to exercise wisdom in your contexts.

Jesus and The Book of Proverbs

Just as Jesus being the 'good shepherd' (John 10:11, 14) enriches the reading of Psalm 23 for the Christian, so Jesus being one 'greater than Solomon' (Matthew 12:42) enriches our reading of the book of Proverbs. The call to live wisely in God's world is as significant today as it was in Old Testament times, but for Christians is focused on the person and work of Jesus, who embodies wisdom in himself. The way of life that flows from the fear of the Lord is found in our following of Jesus, the one who makes it possible to walk the path of wisdom in our everyday life.

Offered a promotion –
what would you do?

JAKE'S STORY

—

Jake was a few years into his civil service career, and out of the 50 or so staff who worked in that office, he was the only 'known' Christian. During this time, his small group were working through a course that explored the way Christian faith can shape workers and workplaces. Through this course, it dawned on him: God really did care about his job. As in actually cared. And not just about him, but his colleagues too. In light of this truth, Jake's conscious desire to honour God in his workplace blossomed.

Not long after the course had finished, Jake was offered a promotion.

While taking the promotion would have meant greater responsibility and financial reward, it also meant moving to a new office. When faced with a decision like this, a wise person factors in the possibilities a new opportunity might bring, as well as the benefits that more money will mean for themselves and for others.

But they weren't the only things Jake took into account. He also thought about the relationships he had with his colleagues; as he contemplated these, he had a strong sense that God was calling him to stay put. He sensed that God wanted him to develop and deepen these relationships, and through them help others to see the reality of Christ and his kingdom.

So, he decided to stay. Not because promotions are bad, nor because moving on is wrong, but because he wanted to honour what he sensed God was calling him to do in that particular season of his life.

What is the outline of the book of Proverbs?

The title in Proverbs 1:1 connects the book to Solomon, even though it's clear from elsewhere in the book that others contributed to the final collection. Headings used throughout the book help us see its overall structure.

1:1-7 Prologue
These opening verses give us the title, an introduction to the book, and the first principle of wisdom – 'The fear of the LORD' (1:7).

1:8–9:18 Speeches
After the prologue, chapters 1–9 contain a series of speeches addressed to a young man encouraging him to pursue wisdom. There are two main voices in this section – that of a parent or parents, and that of Wisdom personified as a woman.

10–24 The Proverbs of Solomon
The title in 10:1 shows this as the start of a new section. It's the first collection of proverbial sayings associated with Solomon, whether written by him or gathered by him or belonging to his collection. It appears to contain separate subsections, with 22:17–24:22 and 24:23–34 marked out as collections of 'sayings of the wise' (22:17; 24:23).

25–29 More Proverbs of Solomon
Chapters 25–29 are a second collection of proverbs associated with Solomon, but said to be 'compiled by the men of Hezekiah king of Judah' (25:1). Here again is an indication that, even if Solomon was the author of many of the proverbs, the book as we have it is a compilation put together after his death.

30 The Sayings of Agur
Chapter 30 then starts a new section with 'the sayings of Agur' (30:1).

31:1-9 The Sayings of King Lemuel
Then we have some 'sayings of King Lemuel', taught by his mother (31:1), which reminds us of the parental instruction of chapters 1–9.

31:10-31 The Grand Finale
Finally, comes a poem about a woman who 'fears the LORD' (31:30). Some consider this passage to be part of the sayings of King Lemuel's mother, whereas others see it as a separate poem in its own right. In either case, far from being a mere appendix about the ideal wife, it brings us back to the personification of Wisdom in the opening chapters of the book, and presents wisdom embodied in the form of a God-fearing woman.

Session 2

A Path to Take

Proverbs 2:1–22

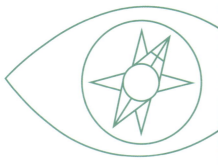

First Thoughts

It looked good to us.

The path was well-trodden and seemed to be heading the right way. Some of us even thought it could be a shortcut to the top of the mountain we were climbing. Hours later, and miles off course, we had to admit we'd gone wrong. This path was going in a completely different direction, and so were we.

The book of Proverbs knows this to be true of life, and sees the stakes as much higher and with significantly greater consequences. So it is that the father instructs his son to walk the way of wisdom which leads to life and avoid the way of folly which leads to death. Proverbs commends to us paths which are marked by the fear of the Lord, and does so by reinforcing the benefits that come to us when we walk in his way. Walking this path helps us navigate the competing perspectives we encounter in everyday life, and enables us to understand the world God has made and how best to live in it.

Read – Proverbs 2:1-22

¹My son, if you accept my words and store up my commands within you, ² turning your ear to wisdom and applying your heart to understanding – ³ indeed, if you call out for insight and cry aloud for understanding, ⁴ and if you look for it as for silver and search for it as for hidden treasure, ⁵ then you will understand the fear of the LORD and find the knowledge of God. ⁶ For the LORD gives wisdom; from his mouth come knowledge and understanding. ⁷ He holds success in store for the upright, he is a shield to those whose way of life is blameless, ⁸ for he guards the course of the just and protects the way of his faithful ones. ⁹ Then you will understand what is right and just and fair – every good path. ¹⁰ For wisdom will enter your heart, and knowledge will be pleasant to your soul. ¹¹ Discretion will protect you, and understanding will guard you. ¹² Wisdom will save you from the ways of wicked men, from men whose words are perverse, ¹³ who have left the straight paths to walk in dark ways, ¹⁴ who delight in doing wrong and rejoice in the perverseness of evil, ¹⁵ whose paths are crooked and who are devious in their ways. ¹⁶ Wisdom will save you also from the adulterous woman, from the wayward woman with her seductive words, ¹⁷ who has left the partner of her youth and ignored the covenant she made before God. ¹⁸ Surely her house leads down to death and her paths to the spirits of the dead. ¹⁹ None who go to her return or attain the paths of life. ²⁰ Thus you will walk in the ways of the good and keep to the paths of the righteous. ²¹ For the upright will live in the land, and the blameless will remain in it; ²² but the wicked will be cut off from the land, and the unfaithful will be torn from it.

Mick Castle
Life is
a refiner.

Focus on the Theme

1. What advice do you recall your parents or grandparents or older friends or mentors giving you?

What favourite sayings have stuck with you over the years?

What Does the Bible Say?

2. Proverbs 2:1-4 describes the search for wisdom, but what (according to 2:5-8) is the goal of the search?

3. What benefits come with knowing God and the wisdom he provides (2:9-11)?

4. What two types of snare does wisdom save us from (2:12-19)?

5. How does wisdom protect us (2:20-22)?

The speeches In Proverbs 1–9

After the introduction in Proverbs 1:1-7 comes a series of speeches addressed to a son by a parent, which extends from 1:8 all the way through to the end of chapter 9. As it happens, there are two main voices in these opening chapters – the voice of the parent, and the voice of Wisdom who is personified as a woman. We're introduced to both in chapter 1 – the parent in 1:9-19 and Woman Wisdom in 1:20-33 – and these two voices then intertwine throughout the rest of the opening section. Much of the instruction in these chapters seems to be aimed at a young man who is just stepping into the adult world. Drawing on the metaphors of two ways, two women, and two houses, the young man is called on to choose – as he sets out on the journey of life – between wisdom and folly.

Going Deeper

6. Some parts of this chapter urge us to look for and search for wisdom (2:4) while other parts say that 'the LORD gives wisdom' (2:5). So, is this wisdom from God discovered by us after a search or given to us as a gift?

7. Glance through Proverbs chapters 3–9 noticing the occasions where the parental address, 'My son', is used (often at the start of a new section). As time allows, read 1:8-19 or 3:11-26 or 4:1-27 and try to spot the similarities as well as any differences with the instruction in Proverbs 2. What might be the reasons for the repetition?

Living it Out

8. What might prevent us from looking for wisdom 'as for silver' and searching for it 'as for hidden treasure' (2:4)? And what would help us in our quest?

9. Think about the ways that any negative influences in our surrounding culture (the equivalent of the 'wicked men' of 2:12 and the 'adulterous woman' of 2:16) affect the environment on your frontline. What do we learn from this passage in Proverbs about how to remain faithful to God and shape the culture of our frontline in positive ways?

10. In the light of this passage, what can you start doing that will help you cultivate understanding and wisdom for your everyday life?

To what extent has the Bible passage or this study helped you to begin to address the issue you highlighted in the opening session?

Prayer Time

- Give thanks that God cares for you and wants you to be wise in order to live well in his world.

- Give thanks that he has given his people wisdom to live by and promises to give it generously to those who ask (James 1:5).

- Pray that your longing for this type of wisdom will be an ongoing feature of your lives, as individuals in your various contexts, and as a church community.

- Pray for those who, for whatever reason, may be struggling to see how God's wisdom makes sense of their lives at the moment.

The different voices of wisdom

On the face it the book of Proverbs appears to be full of confident assertions about life and the consequences of living a certain way. Ecclesiastes and Job belong to the same biblical wisdom tradition, however, and they tell a different story!

Ecclesiastes relates how 'the Teacher, son of David, king of Jerusalem' (1:1) set out to explore every dimension of existence 'under the sun'. Except that no matter what area he examined, the conclusion was always the same – it was 'meaningless' (1:2, 14). The NIV's 'meaningless' translates a Hebrew word which is used 38 times in the book, carrying the idea of vapour or breath; it describes how life is temporary or fleeting – like a mist, here today and gone tomorrow. If any resolution is present in the book, it's found in the closing verses in coming back to the starting point of wisdom – the fear of the Lord (12:13-14). Along the way, we read of the teacher's wrestlings with the meaning of life, and we might well sympathise if we have struggled in similar ways.

Likewise, the book of Job provides a different melody to the seeming confidence of Proverbs. Job's sympathisers draw on conventional wisdom that God will bless those who are good and judge those who do evil. On this basis, they conclude Job is suffering because he has done something wrong, whereas Job insists he hasn't. And that's precisely his dilemma: his suffering has turned his worldview upside-down. As it turns out, the significance of the book lies not in what it says about suffering, but in what it teaches us about God and our relationship with him.

Biblical wisdom, then, requires all these different voices in order to reflect the range and richness of human experience in God's world.

How does Proverbs fit into the Bible as a whole?
————

It sometimes comes as a surprise for readers of Scripture to learn that the book of Proverbs hardly ever refers to major themes of the Bible such as covenant, redemption, law, kingship, and temple. But, given that 'the fear of the LORD is the beginning of wisdom' (9:10), the whole book presupposes the special relationship established between 'the LORD' (Yahweh – God's covenant name) and his people at Mount Sinai.

Looking Back – Creation
As it turns out, the wisdom spoken of in Proverbs is rooted even further back in the biblical story – in creation. Wisdom belongs to the Lord himself, who exercised his wisdom, understanding, and knowledge in the creation of the world (3:19-20). Proverbs 8 describes God as the builder of creation, who used wisdom (personified in these opening chapters as a woman) to make the world (8:22-31).

God's wisdom is somehow woven into the fabric of the world. And the wisdom used by God in building and sustaining creation is the same wisdom now given to them, to be eagerly desired by his people, in order to live wisely in his world. Wisdom's link with creation reinforces its all-embracing scope.

God's wisdom is not limited to the personal or spiritual realms, but encompasses the whole of life, as the sheer range of the individual proverbs in the book makes clear.

But if the wisdom celebrated in the book of Proverbs looks back to creation, it also looks forward to Christ.

Looking Forward – Christ
The portrayal of God's wisdom in Proverbs influenced the New Testament writers in their presentation of Jesus. Just as wisdom as God's agent was active in creation, so Jesus is God's agent in creation (John 1:1-3; Colossians 1:15-20; Hebrews 1:1-4). Paul writes of 'Christ Jesus, who has become for us wisdom from God' (1 Corinthians 1:30), and of Christ, 'in whom are hidden all the treasures of wisdom and knowledge' (Colossians 2:3).

All the blessings of God's wisdom are now mediated through Jesus, himself the wisdom of God.

Wisdom remains a key feature of the Christian life, as it did for the ancient Israelite, but is now focused on the person and work of Jesus. It is through him that we are able to live in harmony with God and the world he has created. The 'fear of the LORD' and the way of life that flows from it now find their fullest expression in relationship with Christ.

Session 3

A Choice to Make

Proverbs 9:1–18

First Thoughts

Ever been double-booked?

Ever had two invitations come for something taking place at the same time, and you have to choose between them? How do you decide which one to accept? Perhaps it comes down to who the invitation is from, or what the invitation is for. Maybe it's about where the finest food will be served, or the most interesting or influential people will be attending, or which will be the best place to be seen. The concluding part of the first main section of the book of Proverbs closes with two invitations – to dinners like no other, from hostesses like no other, with outcomes like no other. Which will we choose?

Read – Proverbs 9:1-18

---

[1] Wisdom has built her house; she has set up its seven pillars.
[2] She has prepared her meat and mixed her wine; she has
also set her table. [3] She has sent out her servants, and she
calls from the highest point of the city, [4] 'Let all who are simple
come to my house!' To those who have no sense she says, [5]
'Come, eat my food and drink the wine I have mixed. [6] Leave
your simple ways and you will live; walk in the way of insight.'
[7] Whoever corrects a mocker invites insults; whoever rebukes
the wicked incurs abuse. [8] Do not rebuke mockers or they
will hate you; rebuke the wise and they will love you. [9] Instruct
the wise and they will be wiser still; teach the righteous and
they will add to their learning. [10] The fear of the LORD is the
beginning of wisdom, and knowledge of the Holy One is
understanding. [11] For through wisdom your days will be many,
and years will be added to your life. [12] If you are wise, your
wisdom will reward you; if you are a mocker, you alone will
suffer. [13] Folly is an unruly woman; she is simple and knows
nothing. [14] She sits at the door of her house, on a seat at the
highest point of the city, [15] calling out to those who pass by,
who go straight on their way, [16] 'Let all who are simple come
to my house!' To those who have no sense she says, [17] 'Stolen
water is sweet; food eaten in secret is delicious!'
[18] But little do they know that the dead are there, that her
guests are deep in the realm of the dead.

Focus on the Theme

1. Who or what out of the following do you trust to give the most reliable advice?

- Family members
- Friends
- Colleagues
- Politicians
- Teachers
- Magazines
- Church leaders
- Doctors
- News readers
- Social media

At this point, you might like to return to the issue or question you raised at the start of Session 1.

Given your particular set of circumstances, on what basis would you trust the advice of others?

What Does the Bible Say?

2. What are the similarities in the way the two women are presented (9:1-6 and 13-18)?

3. What are the main differences between the two women?

4. What benefits does Woman Wisdom bring to her guests (9:7-12)?

5. Only one building would occupy 'the highest point of the city' (9:4) – the temple – meaning that Woman Wisdom seems to represent God's wisdom, indeed God himself. The location of Woman Folly's house, also 'at the highest point of the city' (9:14), suggests that she represents false gods and goddesses. How does this shape our reading of the chapter and the choice offered to us?

Wisdom for life

———

When God is at the centre of our lives, we don't lose out but are called to a full and fruitful existence. That's the thrust of Proverbs 1–9. It's not a dry, sterile life we're invited into with Woman Wisdom. It's rich and blessed, unlike any other offer we'll ever receive elsewhere. And it's not a life which removes us from the world, but one which calls us to live in the world as those who fear the Lord, wherever he has placed us. Proverbs 1–9 instructs its readers about the nature of wisdom and the benefits it brings, providing a lens through which later chapters are to be understood.

Going Deeper

6. As time allows, read 1:20-33 or 8:1-36. How does the portrayal of Woman Wisdom elsewhere in these opening chapters reinforce the insights gleaned from Proverbs 9?

7. Read Matthew 12:42; 1 Corinthians 1:22-25, 30, and Colossians 2:2-3. In what ways is it significant that Jesus is the ultimate source of wisdom for Christians?

Living it Out

8. Every day we encounter many different voices vying for our attention, telling us how to live our lives. Proverbs 9 boils it down to two – Wisdom and Folly. Is it really that simple? Why or why not?

9. Who do you know on your frontline or wider circle of friends who embodies the qualities of 'Woman Wisdom'?

And in what sets of circumstances have you encountered 'Woman Folly'?

How might you emulate the one and resist the other?

10. Karen overheard some of her colleagues talking about her behind her back, calling her a snob, and accusing her of fawning over the bosses. She's upset and angry, but is not sure whether to confront them, speak to the HR manager, or just leave it alone. Based on our reflections so far what would be the wise thing for Karen to do?

Prayer Time

- Confess the ways in which you are sometimes tempted to follow the way of foolishness, and ask God to give you wisdom.

- Give thanks that God's wisdom calls out and is available to all who choose it.

- Pray specifically for each other's frontline situations – for special wisdom that is needed in order to make particular decisions as well as ongoing wisdom in order to live well in those places.

SEAN'S STORY

He'd been a police officer over ten years, but a Christian less than one. Young in his faith as he was, Sean wanted God's wisdom to live and work well.

Sitting in the passenger seat, blue lights flashing and siren blaring, he and a colleague were heading to one of the hardest situations police have to deal with: a domestic violence incident. A number of 'impact factors' were in play too: the assailant was physically strong, was in familiar territory, had access to weapons, and a history of using them. Containing this combustible cocktail would require a sharp mind and a steady heart. As the response vehicle weaved through traffic, Sean prayed for wisdom and for peace.

As he prayed, an element of the fear lifted from him – he felt a peaceful confidence as the Holy Spirit reminded him that he was there for a reason; that it was God's plan that he was in this place at this time.

When they arrived, both the victim and the perpetrator were still in the house, with the latter clearly in no mood to cooperate. What would you have done?

It was in this very flesh and blood, bricks and mortar moment, that both the wisdom Sean had been growing in, as well as the wisdom that God gives 'on the hoof', were brought to bear.

Within the force, respect can be earned by making a difficult arrest. Though attempting that may have led to a moment of personal glory, it could equally have led to serious

Tempted to be heroic rather than wise?

injuries – to Sean and his colleague, or to one or both of this couple as well. In a moment of clarity, Sean felt that he was able to make a decision that he normally would not have made. With the agreement of his colleague, they decided to withdraw the victim from the scene to guarantee her immediate safety, and return later to arrest the culprit. The prospect of gaining kudos did not cloud his duty to protect.

Some hours later, other colleagues, appropriately prepared, returned to arrest the offender, who by that time was in a much calmer state of mind. When interviewed back at the station, he explained how during the time when Sean was on the scene, he was ready to do 'whatever it would have taken' to get away.

Wisdom's ways 'are pleasant ways, and all her paths are peace' (Proverbs 3:17).

What is the social background of the book of Proverbs?

There's an ongoing discussion among scholars as to whether an official group of wise people composed the material in the book of Proverbs, or whether it originated at grassroots level.

Like their neighbours in the ancient Near East, Israel may have had schools attached to the royal court for the development of the nation's leaders. But an increasing number of scholars suggest that the book of Proverbs can be understood just as readily in the context of the home, with its roots in the everyday insights of 'ordinary' people – in both rural and urban settings.

As we've seen, it's certainly clear that Proverbs 1–9 contain the repeated appeal of a 'father' to a 'son' which earths the instruction in a relationship of some kind. The 'father-son' language could be metaphorical for a teacher-pupil relationship, or it could represent a genuine family relationship, not least because a 'mother' is also mentioned (Proverbs 1:8; 6:20; 30:17; 31:1-9, 26), which is unusual compared to wisdom documents in other cultures of the time. From the very beginning of their existence,

the people of God were called to pass on their faith to subsequent generations. The book of Proverbs may reflect the fact that such education largely took place in the family unit.

Perhaps we needn't pinpoint a single source for wisdom. Every setting of life generates its own reflections on living well. Wisdom emerges within specific contexts and is exercised in specific contexts. Whether it was the home or the court or a mixture of both, there is something about the way this book came together, the factors which provoked it, which points to the opportunity to cultivate wisdom in our own contexts.

Whatever the context, a discipling relationship is in view. There's a concept of discipling built into the relationship between the father and the son, which gives life to the instructions, admonitions, and exhortations. The father figure is also passing on a wider tradition, acknowledging his predecessors, seeing himself as a disciple and then a discipler. The 'learner', for their part, is called on to listen attentively, respond obediently, and assimilate carefully what is taught into their life, with the goal of the formation of godly character and a life lived in reverence of the covenant Lord.

The grounding of wisdom in real-life contexts encourages us to reflect on how we're learning to be wise in the everyday. The 'passing on' element is a gentle challenge to ask who we might take further in the ways of being wise.

Session 4

A Life to Pursue

Proverbs 15:16–33

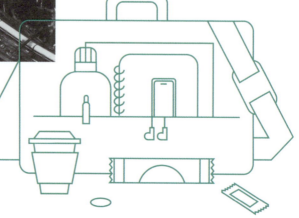

First Thoughts

What collection of issues have you faced today?

Someone in the meeting you were chairing was rude to you. Your deeply-troubled friend called again, the sixth time this week. A difficult family member stretched your patience over dinner. You remembered that you still haven't changed your bank account.

What might wisdom look like in contexts such as these, especially when things don't happen in a predictable order, or when we have to respond in the moment? Proverbs 10–29 is largely a collection of individual proverbial sayings of the sort most often associated with the book. It's sometimes tempting to reorder these, to gather them into distinct themes. This, however, could miss the point that it's their very randomness which makes them especially suitable for reflecting on the way we're often required to negotiate what it means to live wisely in the particularities of daily life. Our lives aren't divided into neat and tidy segments. God doesn't want us to be wise in only one topic, in only one area of life, but in the whole of life.

Read – Proverbs 15:16–33

¹⁶ Better a little with the fear of the LORD than great wealth with turmoil. ¹⁷ Better a dish of vegetables with love than a fattened calf with hatred. ¹⁸ A hot-tempered person stirs up conflict, but the one who is patient calms a quarrel. ¹⁹ The way of the sluggard is blocked with thorns, but the path of the upright is a highway. ²⁰ A wise son brings joy to his father, but a foolish man despises his mother. ²¹ Folly brings joy to one who has no sense, but whoever has understanding keeps a straight course. ²² Plans fail for lack of counsel, but with many advisors they succeed. ²³ A person finds joy in giving an apt reply – and how good is a timely word! ²⁴ The path of life leads upward for the prudent to keep them from going down to the realm of the dead. ²⁵ The LORD tears down the house of the proud, but he sets the widow's boundary stones in place. ²⁶ The LORD detests the thoughts of the wicked, but gracious words are pure in his sight. ²⁷ The greedy bring ruin to their households, but the one who hates bribes will live. ²⁸ The heart of the righteous weighs its answers, but the mouth of the wicked gushes evil. ²⁹ The LORD is far from the wicked, but he hears the prayer of the righteous. ³⁰ Light in a messenger's eyes brings joy to the heart, and good news gives health to the bones. ³¹ Whoever heeds life-giving correction will be at home among the wise. ³² Those who disregard discipline despise themselves, but the one who heeds correction gains understanding. ³³ Wisdom's instruction is to fear the LORD, and humility comes before honour.

Focus on the Theme

1. Take a look at some English proverbs:

- A bird in the hand is worth two in the bush

- Many hands make light work

- Too many cooks spoil the broth

- To kill two birds with one stone

- A rolling stone gathers no moss

Why do you think people made up these sayings?

Why do we still quote them?

In what situations might some of these proverbs be used?

How do we know that the proverbs are true?

Do some proverbs contradict each other, and is it a problem if they do?

What Does the Bible Say?

2. List the sorts of topic covered in these verses. What is your overall impression of the section?

3. Many of the sayings in the book of Proverbs are based on observation of life, the way things usually happen in God's world. What examples can you find of this in Proverbs 15:16–33?

4. Some sayings in the book of Proverbs arise from an understanding of what the Lord is like or how he works. What examples can you find of this in Proverbs 15:16–33?

5. How would you respond to someone who claimed that several of the proverbs in this section appear to promise too much?

What is a proverb?

———

'A proverb is a poetic art form that instills wisdom in you as you wrestle with it.' Timothy Keller with Kathy Keller, *The Way of Wisdom: A Year of Daily Devotions in the Book of Proverbs* (London: Hodder & Stoughton, 2017), vii.

Proverbs are short, pithy, memorable statements, often based on an observation about life, capturing a truth about the way things are meant to work in God's world. They are designed to encourage us to pause and reflect, and to understand the insight or principle embedded in the saying and its implications for our own life and experience. We ask, How does this proverb encourage us to make wise decisions in everyday life? What does it tell us about wise living in the area being spoken about? What pattern does it reveal about the way life tends to work in God's world? What specific actions does it encourage us to adopt or warn us against?

Going Deeper

6. Are the proverbs in this section best seen as statements which are applicable at all times in all circumstances, or as generalisations which are applicable most of the time in many circumstances?

If you can think of 'exceptions' to some of the sayings, what does that say about how we should apply proverbs in our own situations?

7. None of the sayings in this section contain commands, yet they still encourage certain sorts of behaviour or action. For each of the sayings in 15:18-23, what is the proverb requiring you to do, or what kind of person is it calling you to be?

Living it Out

8. In what ways does the apparent randomness of the proverbs in chapters 10–29 inform us about everyday life and wisdom?

9. Which of the individual proverbs explored in this session are particularly relevant to you at the moment, and why?

What might you be able to do this week that will allow you to put the proverbs into practice?

10. Which of the proverbs in this section comes closest to addressing the personal issue or question with which you started this series of studies? How does it help?

Wisdom from Egypt?

Proverbs 22:17–24:22 has some similarity with an Egyptian wisdom text known as the Sayings of Amenemope, usually dated 13th century BC. It's divided into 30 sayings (see 22:20) in which Amenemope instructs his son about not robbing the poor (22:22), not overworking in order to get rich (23:4–5), and not moving ancient landmarks (22:28; 23:10–11), like Proverbs does, with similar wording.

There's a debate about whether the biblical authors 'borrowed' this material, or whether both texts are part of a wider tradition which adapted proven insights about life. But the differences are just as significant: uniquely, Israel saw one God as creator and ruler of all.

God's people were faced with the same issues faced by their neighbours. Since all truth is God's truth, we, like the compilers of Proverbs, might draw genuine insight from 'wisdom' in our wider culture without compromising our faith in the Lord.

Prayer Time

Turn the proverbs in this section into prompts for prayer, asking God to instill his wisdom into your hearts and lives, to help you in any practical decisions you need to take, and to form your character as he does so.

Here's an approach you might like to follow:

- Delegate someone in the group to read two verses at a time.

- Pause for a moment to allow some time to reflect on the verses.

- Offer brief prayers which flow out of those verses. They could be thanksgiving for wisdom, requests for help to live more wisely, or prayers for others. Try to make the prayers specific to your frontline contexts.

Proverbs and character formation

In his book, *The Road to Character,* David Brooks makes a distinction between 'résumé virtues' (the skills which might be listed in your CV) and 'eulogy virtues' (the ones that are talked about at your funeral). Both are important, but the book of Proverbs is mostly interested in the latter.

Character is a way of referring to certain qualities that mark people out. They have to be consistent enough in someone to be counted as traits, and they run through every aspect of life. If I'm kind to my colleagues at work but an ogre with my spouse and children at home, I can't claim to be kind.

Proverbs are designed to cultivate character in the whole of life. The open-ended nature of proverbial sayings requires us to think about where and when they might be applicable, and then calls us to act accordingly. Reading and reflecting on proverbs is not simply about changing isolated incidents of behaviour here and there, but encouraging attitudes that over time become habits which shape our character.

Proverbs

How should we handle individual sayings in Proverbs?

When we read individual proverbs, we're reading the shortest poems in the Bible.

They have qualities of biblical poetry we might be familiar with: short lines, where the second line often reinforces, provides a contrast, or makes more specific the thought of the first line, and a rich use of imagery which invites us to reflect on the point of the comparisons made. Keep a lookout for all these features in your reading of Proverbs.

Proverbs need to be handled carefully, with an appropriate application for different circumstances. Proverbs 26:3 seems to recognise this in describing what's required in order to give direction to a horse and a donkey – what works in one case may not work for the other:

'A whip for the horse, a bridle for the donkey, and a rod for the backs of fools!' (Proverbs 26:3)

The need for a fitting application becomes clear when individual proverbs appear to recommend

different courses of action, as in 26:4-5: 'Do not answer a fool according to his folly, or you yourself will be just like him. Answer a fool according to his folly, or he will be wise in his own eyes.' (Proverbs 26:4-5)

As it happens, the sayings would work on their own if they were isolated from each other; placed side by side, however, they do something more. As the second line in each case indicates, there is wisdom in both courses of action. On the one hand, in responding like a fool, we risk becoming like the fool. On the other hand, it's not always wise to let fools have the last word, in case they mistake their folly for wisdom. All of which is even more significant when there are others around, listening in – during a team meeting, a presentation, or a coffee break conversation. On their own, the pair of proverbs say nothing about the circumstances that require which type of response or even how the 'fool' should be identified. The point is that, at such and such a time one response is to be favoured over the other. Wisdom, in this case, is a matter of what is fitting and what is timely – knowing what to say and when to say it.

The two aphorisms also provide a helpful pointer to how proverbial sayings work more generally. Implicit in the book of Proverbs is the call to live with the ambiguities of life, often in relationship with others, and to navigate wisely through alternate courses of action. In such situations, individual proverbs are not moral absolutes which apply in all circumstances; no one saying contains the whole truth on a particular matter. And so the application of them requires discernment – careful reading of the proverb itself and the situation in which we find ourselves.

Session 5

A Way to Speak

Proverbs
10:18–21
11:11–13
25:11–15
26:17–22

First Thoughts

Words matter.

Alison knew as soon as the words came out of her mouth that she couldn't take them back. Her colleague had said something which put her into fight-or-flight mode, and she ended up fighting. Even if she was right as a matter of principle, she knew she had been right in the wrong way! Her apology to her colleague later that day enabled them to have a more constructive conversation about the issue under discussion.

From the sweet nothings of lovers to the barking commands of generals, words do things. They are powerful tools, with enormous power to tear down or build up, to hurt or heal, to manipulate or mould. No wonder there are more individual proverbs about the tongue than about any other topic. In the everyday contexts in which we find ourselves, when we open our mouths we reveal something of who we are – for good or for ill.

Read – Proverbs
10:18-21; 11:11-13; 25:11-15; 26:17-22

10:18 Whoever conceals hatred with lying lips and spreads slander is a fool. 19 Sin is not ended by multiplying words, but the prudent hold their tongues. 20 The tongue of the righteous is choice silver, but the heart of the wicked is of little value. 21 The lips of the righteous nourish many, but fools die for lack of sense.

11:11 Through the blessing of the upright a city is exalted, but by the mouth of the wicked it is destroyed. 12 Whoever derides their neighbour has no sense, but the one who has understanding holds their tongue. 13 A gossip betrays a confidence, but a trustworthy person keeps a secret.

25:11 Like apples of gold in settings of silver is a ruling rightly given. 12 Like an earring of gold or an ornament of fine gold is the rebuke of a wise judge to a listening ear. 13 Like a snow-cooled drink at harvest time is a trustworthy messenger to the one who sends him; he refreshes the spirit of his master. 14 Like clouds and wind without rain is one who boasts of gifts never given. 15 Through patience a ruler can be persuaded, and a gentle tongue can break a bone.

26:17 Like one who grabs a stray dog by the ears is someone who rushes into a quarrel not their own. 18 Like a maniac shooting flaming arrows of death 19 is one who deceives their neighbour and says, 'I was only joking!' 20 Without wood a fire goes out; without a gossip a quarrel dies down. 21 As charcoal to embers and as wood to fire, so is a quarrelsome person for kindling strife. 22 The words of a gossip are like choice morsels; they go down to the inmost parts.

Focus on the Theme

1. Think of a situation where someone's words harmed you, or, conversely, really encouraged you. In either or both cases, what was it about the words which had that effect?

What Does the Bible Say?

2. List the different types of speech mentioned in these verses.

3. 'The tongue has the power of life and death' (Proverbs 18:21). In what ways, according to the following passages, can words be powerful for good or ill?

- 10:21
- 11:11
- 25:15
- 26:20

4. What metaphors are used in 10:20–21 and 25:11–13 to describe the positive benefits of the words of the righteous?

What images are used in 26:17–22 to describe the negative impact of words wrongfully used?

What are the implications of these metaphors and images?

5. What is the relationship between our speech and our hearts (10:20; see also 15:28; 16:21, 23; 17:20; 26:23–26)?

Going Deeper

6. What does Jesus say about speech in Matthew 12:34–37? Where do our words come from, and what do they reveal about us?

7. How does James' instruction on the use of the tongue (James 3:1–12) cohere with what we have seen in Proverbs?

Proverbial clusters

As we've seen, chapters 10–29 are a collection of sayings of the sort we often associate with the book of Proverbs. They've mostly been read as individual sayings more or less randomly thrown together. However, an increasing number of scholars have been persuaded that there are some clusters of proverbs intentionally grouped around the repetition of words or themes.

So, for instance, 10:1-5 could be seen as a set of proverbs grouped around a contrast between a diligent and a lazy son. Verse 1 and verse 5 contrast two sons, which invites us to read the intervening proverbs in that light. The three sayings in 10:2-4 riff on the acquisition of wealth, suggesting that a family's wellbeing depends, to some extent, on whether children grow up to become workers or wasters. More obvious is 10:18-21 and other passages drawn on in this session, which can be seen as clusters of proverbs on the use of words.

While reading the central sections of the book of Proverbs, it's worth watching out for possible clusters, where the same topic is being addressed, where similar words are used, or where a topic is mentioned only to be dropped and picked up again a few verses later.

Living it Out

8. Think about your own frontline context. In what situations are you most likely to engage in gossip or to quarrel or to lie – at work, among family, with friends, or elsewhere? Why are you tempted to gossip, quarrel, and lie?

9. How do you think others – colleagues, family members, friends – would want you to change your speech?

10. In what specific contexts over the next week will your words carry power or make an impact on others? What strategies might you be able to adopt to be a person of integrity with your words?

Prayer Time

A topic like this one encourages a variety of responses in prayer:

- Thank God for those who have encouraged you with positive words.

- Confess those times when your words to others or about others have been hurtful.

- Request a wise heart so that your words may be used to build others up rather than tear them down.

- Ask for God's help in communicating with others in your different spheres of life – at home, at work, in the cafe, with your aging parents, teenagers, or grandchildren.

Do I need to be male to read the book of Proverbs?

It's easy to see why some have questioned whether the book of Proverbs is 'good news' for women.

On the face of it, many of the exhortations – especially in the opening chapters – are written to a young man on the verge of adulthood. Wisdom takes the form of a father's instruction to a son, and the advice and direction reflect male concerns. The apparently limited portrayal of women in Proverbs has troubled some readers who see women in the book reduced either to temptress or wife.

We should acknowledge that the book in its ancient setting was largely addressed to young men, but there is no implication that women are inferior to men. Alongside warnings about the immoral woman in the opening chapters are the equally clear warnings against men who entice the son into a way that leads to death (e.g. 1:8-19; 2:12-15). In keeping with the rest of the Old Testament, the book warns against illicit sexual relationships, but has no problem with sexual desires appropriately expressed, given the call to the young man to enjoy sexual relations with his wife in Proverbs 5:15-19.

So, even though the book of Proverbs is dominated by a male tone and largely male concerns, it doesn't follow that it is more negative about women than men, or that women shouldn't also be instructed in wise living. In fact, in several places, it is clear that a mother as well as a father is instructing her son (1:8; 6:20; see also 10:1; 15:20; 23:22-25), and King Lemuel passes on instruction given by his mother (30:1-9).

Most significantly of all, perhaps, is that all that is good and life-giving in wisdom is personified as a woman. Proverbs 8 contains the most extensive reflection on the personal nature of wisdom. At the centre of the poem, Woman Wisdom shows her all-embracing significance by affirming her presence at creation, rejoicing in God's presence, and delighting in humankind (8:22-31). The origin of Wisdom from before creation and her presence with the Creator reinforces her claim to be able to provide the benefits mentioned in 8:12-21 and elsewhere. Those who become acquainted with her will be able to navigate life well.

Then, as we will see in our final study, the portrayal of the woman in Proverbs 31:10-31 provides a powerful and fitting crowning point to the teaching about wisdom in the book.

So, while the first readers may well have been primarily male, the wisdom called for by the book of Proverbs is applicable equally to all. Indeed, reading any book of the Bible – whether as men or women – involves an element of imagining ourselves in the place of the original addressees in order to hear the message of the passage before considering what its implications might be in a different historical and cultural setting.

The wisdom of Scripture, including the book of Proverbs, is designed for the whole people of God, men and women.

Session 6

A Model to Follow

Proverbs 31:10–31

First Thoughts

Christ calls us to live our life for him,
but does he really mean all of our life?

And, if he does, what might that look like? We need
wisdom. The beginning of the book of Proverbs
reminds us that wisdom starts with 'fear of the
LORD' (1:7) – the reverent, eager recognition
that the Lord is the source of all true wisdom,
knowledge, and guidance. In the opening chapters,
the father and mother instruct their son setting
out on the path of life, advising him to choose
wisely between the women that will compete for
his affection – Woman Folly and Woman Wisdom.
Then, when we get to the end of the book, we see
that the young man has chosen well! Here is a
snapshot of what a life lived well looks like – in the
portrayal of a woman who 'fears the LORD' (31:30).

Read – Proverbs 31:10–31

[10] A wife of noble character who can find? She is worth far more than rubies. [11] Her husband has full confidence in her and lacks nothing of value. [12] She brings him good, not harm, all the days of her life. [13] She selects wool and flax and works with eager hands. [14] She is like the merchant ships, bringing her food from afar. [15] She gets up while it is still night; she provides food for her family and portions for her female servants. [16] She considers a field and buys it; out of her earnings she plants a vineyard. [17] She sets about her work vigorously; her arms are strong for her tasks. [18] She sees that her trading is profitable, and her lamp does not go out at night. [19] In her hand she holds the distaff and grasps the spindle with her fingers. [20] She opens her arms to the poor and extends her hands to the needy. [21] When it snows, she has no fear for her household; for all of them are clothed in scarlet. [22] She makes coverings for her bed; she is clothed in fine linen and purple. [23] Her husband is respected at the city gate, where he takes his seat among the elders of the land. [24] She makes linen garments and sells them, and supplies the merchants with sashes. [25] She is clothed with strength and dignity; she can laugh at the days to come. [26] She speaks with wisdom, and faithful instruction is on her tongue. [27] She watches over the affairs of her household and does not eat the bread of idleness. [28] Her children arise and call her blessed; her husband also, and he praises her: [29] 'Many women do noble things, but you surpass them all.' [30] Charm is deceptive, and beauty is fleeting; but a woman who fears the LORD is to be praised. [31] Honour her for all that her hands have done, and let her works bring her praise at the city gate.

Focus on the Theme

---

1. Who do we tend to hold up as Christian role models, and why? In what activities are they generally involved?

What Does the Bible Say?

---

2. What areas of life are included in the praise of the woman? What qualities do we see in her?

3. Why is she described as fearing the Lord (31:30) when the passage nowhere shows her engaging in 'religious' activities? In what ways, then, does this woman embody the fear of the Lord?

4. In the opening study, we saw how Proverbs is written for us to receive instruction 'in prudent behaviour, doing what is right and just and fair', and to give 'knowledge and discretion' (1:4-5). How far does the woman in 31:10-31 exemplify prudence, righteousness, and discretion?

5. The book of Proverbs regularly addresses the themes of work, speech, and our relationships with others. How does the portrayal of the woman in this passage cohere with those concerns?

An A to Z of wisdom

Proverbs 31:10–31 has been written as an acrostic poem, with each of the twenty-two verses beginning with a consecutive letter of the Hebrew alphabet, from aleph, the first, to taw, the last, the equivalent of A to Z in English. This suggests we are not necessarily to expect a logical progression through the poem, let alone a 'checklist', but more a range of snapshots that make up the whole picture in which every aspect of her life is marked by the fear of the Lord. It seems appropriate that the woman should be honoured with the use of a carefully crafted literary device, one which shows the full, comprehensive range of her activities and virtues.

A remarkable Woman

Our journey to becoming wise flows out of our relationship with God. The book that begins with the fear of the Lord (1:7) ends with the fear of the Lord (31:10). It is seen exemplified in this portrayal of a woman whose wisdom is demonstrated in her everyday activities of being a wife to her husband, a mother to her children, providing for her family, managing her household, engaging in international trade in cloths and textiles, negotiating the purchase of fields, looking out for the poor, and more besides. Her wisdom is expressed and embodied in her everyday pursuits, in a way which enables others to flourish, and which embraces every aspect of life.

Going Deeper

6. What are the similarities between the woman of this passage and the portrayal of Woman Wisdom in Proverbs 9:1–12? What might this suggest about the identity of the woman in Proverbs 31:10–31?

7. In what ways do James 1:5 and 3:13–18 add to the picture of biblical wisdom that has been emerging in these studies in Proverbs?

Living it Out

8. Proverbs 31:10–31 is less about being a 'good wife' and more about living wisely as women – and men – who fear the Lord. Are you encouraged or intimidated by the portrayal of the person in this passage? In what ways?

9. If applicable, go back to the particular issue that you felt you needed wisdom for at the start of the first session. What inspiration have you been able to draw from the passages in Proverbs looked at during these studies?

10. Reflect back over your studies in the book of Proverbs. What lessons have you found particularly helpful? What changes have you begun to make in your life?

Prayer Time

The passage highlights the significance of ordinary activities and the potential to live 'heroically' in everyday life as those who 'fear the Lord'.

- Read the passage prayerfully, perhaps pausing after every three or four verses to allow reflection and response.

- Thank God for how he has helped you in the areas mentioned, and ask for his help and wisdom for your own activities in the coming weeks.

Epilogue

At the end of this study of Proverbs, try to find a time when you can review the whole study prayerfully before God.

What was the most significant insight for you from the book?

_____

_____

_____

_____

What did you learn about reading Proverbs that you think might help you when you read other wisdom writing in the Bible?

_____

_____

_____

_____

Looking back on what was happening on your frontline when you started, how have you seen God at work?

_____

_____

_____

_____

HAZEL'S STORY

Amidst the munching of cereal and the search for missing PE socks, Hazel helps the kids get ready before her husband takes over the school run.

By 8 o'clock, she's driving the familiar route to the secondary school where she teaches, praying as she goes. She knows she's going to need God's wisdom for whatever this day might bring. She's strengthened as she remembers that her heavenly Father is interested in her, the people she'll be with, the problems she'll need to solve, and the opportunities that might come her way.

Around mid-morning, she meets with a student struggling with friendship issues. With kindness yet truth, she helps this 11-year-old see himself through another's eyes. As he leaves, more hopeful, she thanks God that she managed not to crush him in the process.

In the staff room, a flapping colleague turns to her for help. Hazel spots a way to affirm her capabilities and offer some perspective, before going on to suggest a strategy to de-escalate the situation. She's grateful the colleague confided in her – Hazel knows she was approaching meltdown, and that wouldn't have been good for anyone.

Along the way, of course, she's teaching classes, dealing with the disruptors, encouraging the strugglers, pushing the complacent. She prepares a lesson, recognising the challenges some of her students might have with this particular topic. She even manages a necessary call to a parent, making another small dent in the admin pile on her desk.

How do you bring God into your day?

When she gets home later that day, she dons her 'parent hat', which apparently qualifies her as a taxi driver, mediator, chef, counsellor, and first-aider. She's aware of the opportunities to both model and teach the virtues of patience, kindness, goodness, self-control, and forgiveness. Unnatural grace – where else will her kids experience it as they grow? A few arrow-prayers are shot up along the way.

Once the kids are in bed, she attacks the pile of marking she brought home, knowing the feedback will help her students take another step forward in their grasp of the subject. She treasures a moment with her husband over a cup of tea, chatting about their days: what they've done, what made them smile, what made them sigh, where they've noticed God. It's precious time to catch up and relax – they're not robots. They round off the day with a programme, before calling it a night, knowing that in eight hours it all starts again.

Ordinary day? Or extraordinary day? Hazel will probably not have a book written about her or be mentioned in a sermon. Yet she lives in the 'fear of the Lord', honouring him through serving others in all the 'good work' she seeks to do. 'A woman (or man) who fears the Lord is to be praised.'

Further reading on Proverbs

Further reading on Proverbs for those who might like to dig deeper into the book.

Reading Proverbs with Integrity Grove Biblical Series 22
Craig Bartholomew
Cambridge: Grove Books, 2001

The Fear of the Lord Is Wisdom: A Theological Introduction to Wisdom in Israel
Tremper Longman III
Grand Rapids: Baker Academic, 2017

Proverbs, The Story of God Bible Commentary
Ryan P. O'Dowd
Grand Rapids: Zondervan, 2017

A Life that Is Good: The Message of Proverbs for a World Wanting Wisdom
Glenn Pemberton
Grand Rapids: Eerdmans, 2018

Proverbs: An Introduction and Commentary, Tyndale Old Testament Commentary
Lindsay Wilson
London: IVP, 2017

Other resources from LICC

The One About...

Eight stories about God in our everyday

There is no such thing as an ordinary day for a Christian. With Christ, every day, every task, every relationship brims with divine possibility. God is always at work in our lives. But can we see it?

Suitable for individual reading or group reflection, this inspiring collection of true stories told by Mark Greene, Executive Director of LICC, offers us a window into the rich, varied, and sometimes surprising ways God works in our everyday lives.

licc.org.uk/theoneabout

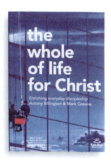

The Whole of Life for Christ

Seven Bible Studies for Individuals and Small Groups

Suppose for a moment that Jesus really is interested in every aspect of your life. This isn't just a nice idea – it's threaded right through the Bible. The deeper we dig into God's word the more we're affirmed in our calling to be disciples of Jesus in every area of our lives.

These seven studies, developed by Antony Billington and Mark Greene in partnership with Keswick Ministries, also include leader's material to inform and prompt group discussion.

licc.org.uk/wlfc

LICC Website

Whether you're looking to grow in your understanding of the Bible and its implications for your daily life, understand how to respond to the pressures and opportunities in today's world or workplace, or looking for resources to help as you lead a whole life disciple-making community, LICC's recently refreshed website is packed full of articles, videos, stories, and resources to help you on your journey.

Visit licc.org.uk

About LICC

What difference does following Jesus make to our ordinary Monday to Saturday lives out in God's world? And how can we bring his wisdom, hope, grace, and truth to the things we do every day, to the people we're usually with, and the places we naturally spend time?

Vital questions in any era. After all, the 98% of UK Christians who aren't in church-paid work spend 95% of their time away from church, much of it with the 94% of our fellow citizens who don't know Jesus. Tragically, most Christians in the UK don't feel equipped to make the most of those opportunities. But what if they were?

That's what we at LICC are seeking to achieve. We work with individuals, church leaders, and theological educators from across the denominations. We delve into the Bible, think hard about the culture we're in, listen carefully to God's people, explore their challenges and opportunities... And we pray, write, speak, train, consult, research, develop, and test resources that offer the biblical frameworks, the lived examples, the practical skills, and the spiritual practices that enable God's people to know him more richly in their everyday lives, and grow as fruitful, whole-life followers of Christ right where they are, on their everyday frontlines, to the glory of God, and the blessing and salvation of many.

To find out more, including ways you can receive news of our latest resources, events, and articles, by email or post, go to licc.org.uk

licc.
The London Institute for
Contemporary Christianity